We Live In Upside Down Land

By Publius Marcus

Matthew 25:41; "Then shall he say also unto them on the left hand, Depart from me, ye cursed, into everlasting fire, prepared for the devil and his angels:"

Ecclesiastes 10:2; "A wise man's heart is at his right hand; but a fool's heart at his left."

COPYRIGHT

CONTENTS

Opening statement

The Snooper Report was at one time one of the most prestigious conservative blogs on the Internet. It followed the Other John McCain's ten most popular items to get over 1 million readers and the plan worked for nearly 2 years. The Alexa Ratings approached the 90,000 mark for a few years and now it is at almost 9 million in the ratings. I don't care.

The interest of The Snooper Report now is promoting Jesus Christ, which it should have been doing since it began.

The Snooper Report eventually started at Townhall and that blog was in the Top Ten there for well over a year. After much tomfoolery there, it went to Wordpress. From Wordpress it went to Blogger. Via the "multitudinal " lunacy from the libtards via the democrats, socialists, communists and republicans, I decided to get my own web site. I approached many and I found Squarespace as my new home.

I placed everything from Townhall, Wordpress and Blogger at The Snooper Report and all was well from the Moonbat fruit loop brigades from all political parties. Yes they made retarded comments and I made blog posts out if their comments. Cutting a long story short, I was wasting my time trying to correct these satanic dunderheads and the more angry I got, it gave me medical problems.

I write books about God now and all is well with my soul. Satan hates it but he is an idiot so, oh well. God is pleased with me now and my books are now published.

Chapter 1: Live Free or Die Trying[1,2,3]

Disclaimer: I do not hate Barack Hussein Obama. (disclaimer presented here so some idiot of the Moonbat Fruit Loop Brigades that claims that I do will get trounced and treated as the slime balls that they are). This Disclaimer was inspired by Duane Lester so, moving on...

"I want Barack Hussein Obama to fail and fail miserably. He is already Carteresque so he might as well complete the cycle as the worst President Marxist in history. I want him to fail so miserably that by the time he is either found to be ineligible to be in the White Marxist House, impeached, run out of town on a rail or gets horribly defeated in 2012, he is 5 feet shorter than he is at the moment and he has a head of hair grayer than gray and he needs a walker to exit stage left. And he can take his disbarred tag-along with him, too.

His "transition team" is nothing more than an Americanized cabal of the Soviet Politburo. Corruption is their game."

If Obama is allowed to succeed, the Nation falls. I have yet to see any references to the United States Constitution that supports and reconciles his proposed Plan(s). The same goes for both Houses of CONgress, R, D or I. Period. I triple-dog dare anyone to present in the comments section the Constitutional chapter and verse, which supports ANYTHING the Marxicrats, (R, D or I) has been presenting in CONgress.

Bring it.

Live Free Or Die.

Oklahoma. New Hampshire. These two States demand their State Sovereignty returned to them.

Oklahoma:

"The resolution's language, in part, reads: "Whereas, the 10th Amendment to the Constitution of the United States reads as follows: 'The powers not delegated to the United States by the Constitution, nor prohibited by it to the States, are reserved to the States respectively, or to the people'; and Whereas, the 10th Amendment defines the total scope of federal power as being that specifically granted by the Constitution of the United States and no more; and whereas, the scope of power defined by the 10th Amendment means that the federal government was created by the states specifically to be an agent of the states; and Whereas, today, in 2008, the states are demonstrably treated as agents of the federal government. ... Now, therefore, be it resolved by the House of Representatives and the Senate of the 2nd session of the 51st Oklahoma Legislature: that the State of Oklahoma hereby claims sovereignty under the 10th Amendment to the Constitution of the United States over all powers not otherwise enumerated and granted to the federal government by the Constitution of the United States. That this serve as Notice and Demand to the federal government, as our agent, to cease and desist, effective immediately, mandates that are beyond the scope of these constitutionally delegated powers." Key's resolution passed in the Oklahoma House of Representatives with a 92 to 3 vote, but it reached a bottleneck in the Senate where it languished until adjournment. However, Key plans to reintroduce the measure when the Legislature reconvenes."

New Hampshire:

HCR-6 New Hampshire Bill to reassert State Sovereignty.

"The People of the Nation-State of New Hampshire as defined in the Articles of Confederation are asserting their right to Nation State-hood Sovereignty with Bill HCR-6. This legislation intends to reverse the erroneous conclusions of the Supreme court and the Federal Government as a whole that the Federal Government is the supreme authority and law of the land. This legislation is the first step towards putting the federal government back on it's lease as a servant of the Sovereign inhabitants of the several Nation-states; not the subject/Citizens of the Corporate UNITED STATES. Americans are a free people with no reservations created through BAR attorneys operation for the interests of the City of London. Leading by example the people of New Hampshire have boldly put the federal government on notice with HCR 6 - A Resolution affirming States' rights based on Jeffersonian principles."

And here we have the beginnings of telling the "elected cockroaches" in DC where to stick their multitude of Big Brother intrusions. Screw DC. The vast majority of the American Electorate are flat-out dumb. They do not know their Constitutions, both State or Federal. It isn't taught anywhere anymore and they listen to the politicians talk about the Constitution and seen to trust them. Those of us that have studied the Founding Documents for decades see what is happening and this is why I write and network like crazy.

9

Pay attention people.

I want the 111th Congress to fail.

I want Obama to fall flat on his morphed Marxism (Americanized Marxism - Stalin, Lenin, Chairman Mao, Engels and Marx) face. Period. I do not recognize his authority nor will I abide by any unconstitutional idiocy oozing from the pits of the very dishonorable void-of-understanding halls of CONgress. Period.

Texas is ripe to secede and I am all for it.

Long live the Republic of Texas, the Lone Star State.

Virginia Rebel - US Civil Flags -

On today's show, it was asserted that 9 States have done the same and they are: nine states (WA, AZ, MT, MI, MO, OK, CA, GA) are following NH's lead by claiming their "sovereignty" under the 10th Amendment.

Found at South Carolina League of the South (Take Down That Flag). It is "nice" that these States are claiming their Independence but as they say at SCLotS, when there is no follow through, what good is it? (Colorado, Alaska, and Georgia)

Washington - Washington State Legislature - HJM 4009 - 2009-10

Arizona - HCR 2024 - State of Arizona, House of Representatives, Forty-ninth Legislature, First Regular Session, 2009

Montana - 2009 Montana Legislature, HOUSE BILL NO. 246

Michigan - House Concurrent Resolution No. 4

Missouri - HR 212 - Declares Missouri's sovereignty under the Tenth Amendment and urges the United States Congress to reject the passage of the federal Freedom of Choice Act which prohibits regulations on abortion

Hawaii - (they want to split away)

At this time, I do not have the California or Georgia links. New Hampshire and Oklahoma legislation is in the body of the post above.

So far, in totality, there are 9 States that have legislation and if I can find CA and GA, that will be 11.

I learned a few hours ago that the Republic of Texas has leapt into the fray.

HALLELUJAH! I am a Texican and a member of the Republic of Texas. We have been working on this for almost forever and it is finally coming around the bend. The next step is Secession but we may not have to go that far. Not if this initiative is carried through all the way. Anything shy of full State Sovereignty is unacceptable.

As a fellow member at the American Daily Review stated:

This week my home state of Texas joined the anti-socialist movement that is sweeping the nation by telling the Federal government to take a hike. Joining with the other sovereign state legislation, Texas Representative Brandon Creighton filed a concurrent resolution, which states the following:

Currently, there are 19 States telling the Czar to kiss our ass.
Last Change: 02/19/09

Arizona: (02/10/09)
Arizona State Reps and Senators Introduce Citizenship Bill
AZ State Reps Introduce State Sovereignty Resolution

Colorado: (12/16/08)
Candidate Qualification: CO Legislative Council Begins Ballot Initiative Process
Ballot Initiative to Certify Candidate Eligibility Submitted in Colorado

Georgia: (02/18/09)
GA State Reps Introduce State Sovereignty Resolution; Neal Boortz and the 10th Amendment Commission

From Georgia: Georgia Constitutional Convention and the Fair Tax, School

Vouchers, Proof of Citizenship to Vote

Massachusetts: (02/06/09)
MA Concerned Citizen Submits State Sovereignty Bill to State Rep

Michigan: (02/04/09)
MI State Rep Introduces Resolution on State Sovereignty

Mississippi: (02/13/09)
MS State Senator Authors Bill Protecting Gun Owners During Martial Law

Missouri: (02/04/09)
MO State Reps Propose State Sovereignty Bill Regarding FOCA

Montana: (02/04/09)
MT State Rep Introduces Bill to Exempt Firearms from Federal Regulation (2nd and 10th Amendments)

New Hampshire: (02/17/09)
Glenn Beck Covers NH Sovereignty Resolution, OK State Rep Editorial
NH State Reps Introduce Bill Reaffirming States' Rights

North Dakota: (01/22/09)
State Initiative Update: ND, UT Considering Legislation to Modify Statutes

Ohio: (02/07/09)
OH Blogger Working to Get State Sovereignty Resolution Introduced
OH State Rep Offers Joint Resolution Asking Electoral College to Confirm Citizenship

Oklahoma: (02/18/09)
OK 10th Amendment Resolution Passes State House 83-13
Glenn Beck Covers NH Sovereignty Resolution, OK State Rep Editorial
Oklahoma Citizenship Bill Passes Committee
Making it Easier to Petition the Government
OK State Rep to Reintroduce State Sovereignty Bill
Ballot Update: OK State Rep Ritze Pre-fills Bill
OK State Rep to Introduce Bill Requiring Documentation for Ballot Placement

Pennsylvania: (02/13/09)
PA State Rep To Introduce State Sovereignty Resolution
PA State Rep Authoring Legislation on Candidate Eligibility Based on Obama Citizenship Questions

South Carolina: (02/17/09)
SC Reps Introduce State Sovereignty Bill

Tennessee: (02/19/09)
TN State Rep Introduces State Sovereignty Resolution
WND: More TN Lawmakers Sign Up for Eligibility Lawsuit
TN Representative Agrees to be Plaintiff on Eligibility, Proposes Sovereignty Bill

Texas: (02/18/09)
TX State Rep Introduces State Sovereignty Resolution

Utah: (02/11/09)
UT State Rep Introduces Bill Opting State Out of REAL ID Act (10th Amendment)
State Initiative Update: ND, UT Considering Legislation to Modify Statutes

Virginia: (02/13/09)
VA REAL ID Bill Readied for Governor's Signature

Washington: (02/04/09)
WA State Reps Introduce Bill on State Sovereignty

UPDATE! Minnesota has chimed in. This makes 20 States now.

H.F. 997: Minnesota Joins State Sovereignty Movement!
Posted by North Star Liberty on 02/19/09 12:55PM. This bill

was introduced this morning into the MN House of Representatives. It is currently supported by 16 State Representatives. As with other states attempting to reassert the power of the 10th Amendment, it seeks to affirm our long diminished state sovereignty against the overwhelming mandates of the Federal government. I hope we Minnesotan liberty lovers can get behind this!

Here we go folks! It's about time, too.

The Chicago Tea Party? What's next? The Fargo Tea Party? What ever city chooses to have their version of the original Boston Tea Party, the better off the Nation will be. The trolls that wander the Dishonorable Halls of CONgress, echoing their chants of "I Won" need to be stopped dead in their tracks.

The intellectual malfeasance and the unconstitutional mantra of "The Will of The Congress Will Be Done" needs to be exorcised.

Macsmind says:

"It's a good point though. How many of you are happy - even if you don't own a house - are now going to help pay for the houses of those who by their own choice and stupidity got into a mortgage they couldn't afford? I'm about to head to the docks now."

Live free or die trying is the American Patriot's lead.

I will end this chapter with the following citation from a good friend of mine by the name of Dean...wherever he is right now:

"For so long as there shall but one hundred of us remain alive we will never give consent to subject ourselves to the dominion of anti-American Marxists, neither shall we bow to the rule of despots and from our knees beg for our lives. For it is not glory, it is not riches, neither is it honours, but it is liberty alone that we fight and contend for, which no honest man will lose but with his life. We, the Remnant, the Patriot, shall stand on our feet and fight for our God given right to be free men and women." ~Dean~[6]

So what does the Scripture say about living free? The Scriptures have a plethora of topics on this subject but I will be brief. I know. I won't post the verses that you know about but that's just the way that it is.

Seeing that we are following the Constitution and that Constitution was freely given to this nation, aren't we all the servants of the Lord? Now, naturally, the unsaved either don't know this or choose to not follow it, it leaves the followers of Jesus Christ to follow **1 Corinthians 7:22**, "*For he that is called in the Lord, being a servant, is the Lord's freeman: likewise also he that is called, being free, is Christ's servant.*" There are many other verses to look into and study but doesn't this verses, in this passage, inform us that Freedom equates to belief in Jesus Christ?

Doesn't Jesus Christ say that truth sets us free or does He say that at first one must know the truth? **John 8:32**, "*And ye shall know the truth, and the truth shall make you free.*"

What do we know as truth considering what this nation was steeped upon in comparison to any socialist/communist nation? It doesn't take much of an imagination, a child's imagination, to know that our freedom is vested upon and within a belief in Jesus Christ.

Just so you will know, the terms "free", "freed", "freedmen" (libertines), "freedom", "freely" and "freemen", there are 83 verses of Scripture given. Study those and what you find is that the current crop of dunderheads driving this nation into that abyss of obscurity are exactly that – dunderheads.

So, what did the Holy Spirit say about one's own country?

Matthew 13:53-58; "And it came to pass, that when Jesus had finished these parables, he departed thence. And when he was come into his own country, he taught them in their synagogue, insomuch that they were astonished, and said, Whence hath this man this wisdom, and these mighty works? Is not this the carpenter's son? is not his mother called Mary? and his brethren, James, and Joses, and Simon, and Judas? And his sisters, are they not all with us? Whence then hath this man all these things? And they were offended in him. But Jesus said unto them, A prophet is not without honour, save in his own country, and in his own house. And he did not many mighty works there because of their unbelief."

Mark 6:1-6; "And he went out from thence, and came into his own country; and his disciples follow him. And when the sabbath day was come, he began to teach in the synagogue: and many hearing him were astonished, saying, From whence hath this man these things? and what wisdom is this which is given unto him, that even such mighty works are wrought by his hands? Is not this the carpenter, the son of Mary, the brother of James, and Joses, and of Juda, and Simon? and are not his sisters here with us? And they were offended at him. But Jesus, said unto them, A prophet is not without honour, but in his own country, and among his own kin, and in his own house. And he could there do no mighty work, save that he laid his hands upon a few sick folk, and healed them. And he marvelled because of their unbelief. And he went round about the villages, teaching."

Luke 4:16-29; "And he came to Nazareth, where he had been brought up: and, as his custom was, he went into the synagogue on the sabbath day, and stood up for to read. And there was delivered unto him the book of the prophet Esaias. And when he had opened the book, he found the place where it was written, The Spirit of the Lord is upon me, because he hath anointed me to preach the gospel to the poor; he hath sent me to heal the brokenhearted, to preach deliverance to the captives, and recovering of sight to the blind, to set at liberty them that are bruised, To preach the acceptable year of the Lord. And he closed the book, and he gave it again to the minister, and sat down. And the eyes of all them that were in the synagogue were fastened on him. And he began to say unto them, This day is this scripture fulfilled in your ears. And all bare him witness, and wondered at the gracious words which proceeded out of his mouth. And they said, Is not this Joseph's son? And he said unto them, Ye will surely say unto me this proverb, Physician, heal thyself: whatsoever we have heard done in Capernaum, do also here in thy country. And he said, Verily I say unto you, No prophet is accepted in his own country. But I tell you of a truth, many widows were in Israel in the days of Elias, when the heaven was shut up three years and six months, when great famine was throughout all the land; But unto none of them was Elias sent, save unto Sarepta, a city of Sidon, unto a woman that was a widow. And many lepers were in Israel in the time of Eliseus the prophet; and none of them was cleansed, saving Naaman the Syrian. And all they in the synagogue, when they heard these things, were filled with wrath, And rose up, and thrust him out of the city, and led him unto the brow of the hill whereon their city was built, that they might cast him down headlong."

John 4:43-45; "Now after two days he departed thence, and went into Galilee. For Jesus himself testified, that a prophet hath no honour in his own country. Then when he was come into Galilee, the Galilaeans received him, having seen all the things that he did at Jerusalem at the feast: for they also went unto the feast."

Are we "constitutionalists" the accepted practice in this land or are we "constitutionalists" the rejected for a "more better union"?

Chapter 2: Titles of Nobility and Honor - The Missing 13th Amendment[4]

The following is an article that I wrote about many moons ago on a different web site, which no longer exists. So, here it is one more time.

"In the winter of 1983, archival research expert David Dodge, and former Baltimore police investigator Tom Dunn, were searching for evidence of government corruption in public records stored in the Belfast Library on the coast of Maine. By chance, they discovered the library's oldest authentic copy of the Constitution of the United States (printed in 1825). Both men were stunned to see this document included a 13th Amendment that no longer appears on current copies of the Constitution. Moreover, after studying the Amendment's language and historical context, they realized the principle intent of this "missing" 13th Amendment was to prohibit lawyers from serving in government.

So began a seven-year, nationwide search for the truth surrounding the most bizarre Constitutional puzzle in American history — the unlawful removal of a ratified Amendment from the Constitution of the United States.

Since 1983, Dodge and Dunn have uncovered additional copies of the Constitution with the "missing" 13th Amendment printed in at least eighteen separate publications by ten different states and territories over four decades from 1822 to 1860.

In June of this year, Dodge uncovered the evidence that this missing 13th Amendment had indeed been lawfully ratified by the state of Virginia and was therefore an authentic Amendment to the American Constitution. If the evidence is correct and no logical errors have been made, a 13th Amendment restricting lawyers from serving in government was ratified in 1819 and removed from our Constitution during the tumult of the Civil War. Since the Amendment was never lawfully repealed, it is still the Law today. The implications are enormous. The story of this "missing" Amendment is complex and at times confusing because the political issues and vocabulary of the American Revolution were different from our own. However, there are essentially two issues: What does the Amendment mean and, was the Amendment ratified? Before we consider the issue of ratification, we should first understand the Amendment's meaning and consequent current relevance."

The link offers the wherewithal for all to read. It was written in 1991 and that's a long time ago.

There are many trains of thought about the alleged 13th Amendment and the current 13th Amendment. Those that argue that the AWOL 13th Amendment is a myth are the actual myth talkers themselves and are, in fact, part of the American Leftinistra. Do your own searches. I have. Rely on no one else. Come up with your own factual accounts and you can start be researching your own State. As for the ratification of the "original" 13th Amendment, it was in fact fully ratified by 1812...the War of 1812 was when?

Now, oddly enough and I do mean "oddly", the Daily Kos has a very good rendering on the lost 13th Amendment. The "Missing" 13th Amendment, an odd Constitution story. This article was written by Pinche Tejano on 7.10.2007 so the story is in fact old.

Many of us have looked into this missing 13th Amendment but the lawyers will not hear of it. So what does the 13th Amendment, as originally published, have to say?

"If any citizen of the United States shall accept, claim, receive, or retain any title of nobility or honour, *or* shall without the consent of Congress, accept and retain any present, pension, office, or emolument of any kind whatever, from any emperor, king, prince, or foreign power, *such person shall cease to be a citizen of the United States*, and *shall be incapable of holding any office of trust or profit under them*, or either of them", emphasis mine.

An attorney, on their sheepskin diploma, there is a word and that word is Esquire, and that term is a British term of British Nobility.

Interesting. I wonder why the lawyers were going to be forbidden? And why was this removed and replaced with the current version? Was there some Leftinistra tomfoolery going on? Considering that the attorneys in DC, as our "illustrious leaders", are screwing up the nation, no wonder they did away with the "original" 13th amendment.

Good site: War Records: War Department document from 1825 reveals critical clue to missing 13th Amendment

Like I have stated many times...do your own research. For years I thought all of this was a rude hoax. And I was wrong.

And, I will end with the following but I want you all to think back to what was happening to the world back then. "The meaning of peace is the absence of opposition to socialism." - Karl Marx, German political Philosopher and revolutionary, 1818-1883.

What has bothered me the most about this "hiding" of the original and truly ratified document known as the Original 13th Amendment, after I figured all of this out, is the following: **Isaiah 29:15**, "*Woe unto them that seek deep to hide their counsel from the LORD, and their works are in the dark, and they say, Who seeth us? and who knoweth us?*" Read that entire chapter in Isaiah and you tell me what you think.

Hasn't this truth been much talked about and haven't we been hearing that all of this is really "out there"? So, after reading the entire chapter 29 in the Book of Isaiah, what in the world was going on in the mind of the Prophet Jeremiah?

Jeremiah 23:23-29, "*Am I a God at hand, saith the LORD, and not a God afar off? Can any hide himself in secret places that I shall not see him? saith the LORD. Do not I fill heaven and earth? saith the LORD. I have heard what the prophets said, that prophesy lies in my name, saying, I have dreamed, I have dreamed. How long shall this be in the heart of the prophets that prophesy lies? yea, **they are prophets of the deceit of their own heart**; Which think to cause my people to forget my name by their dreams which they tell every man to his neighbour, as their fathers have **forgotten my name for Baal**. The prophet that hath a dream, let him tell a dream; and he that hath my word, let him speak my word faithfully. What is the chaff to the wheat?*"

saith the LORD. **Is not my word like as a fire?** *saith the LORD; and like a hammer that breaketh the rock in pieces?"*

This subterfuge and destruction of this Amendment by the "attorneys" of this land (think back to 1871) is tantamount to bordering on blasphemy, the unforgiveable or unpardonable sin. I will not be getting into the seven deadly sins or really getting into the true meanings of blasphemy, but I do wish to inform you that the "unpardonable" or "unforgiveable" sin can still be witnessed to and actually done in this day and age – and I truly believe that Satan got into the fray of this Constitution through the attorneys and others that tore the original 13th Amendment out and threw in another one in its place some time after the War Between the States was over with.

Mark 3:22-30, Matthew 12:22-32, Mark 3:30, Acts 5:1-10, John 3:16, John 14:6 and 1 John 1:9 more or less explains what blasphemy is and what it means to be accused of this sin.

As far as I am concerned, anything other than the Law of The Land, our Constitution, which is not being followed, is blasphemy because God gave us this Constitution which no one in DC even comes close to following and look what has come of us all.

The tossing aside of the original 13th Amendment with no explanations and without a full ratification, as far as I am concerned, is a treasonous transaction.

Chapter 3: Our founding document wasn't set in stone for a reason₅

The title of this article is from a Leftinistra hack, in all places, Texas. Bob Ray Sanders has been on my hit list for many years but I haven't written about him because his normal antics haven't been worthy of my time. However, this is not the case this time around. If this Leftinistra hack do-nothing nincompoop doesn't think that the United States Constitution wasn't ever set in stone, that means that this cretinous buffoon has never read the documents and thinks that a United States Supreme Court Justice thinks for us all and can make whatever Law they so seem to make. This means that Bob Ray Sanders has never read in the United States Constitution what SCOTUS can and cannot do. But, then again, I guess that's what is wrong with the USC, according to this buffoon from Texas. We need a "New Foundation".

Let's take a look at this buffoonish outtake of the Founding Document of the greatest Nation around even though the Jihadi Obama is running the show - if we can say that without laughing our butts off about it.

"President Barack Obama's latest nominee to the U. S.

Supreme Court is still making the rounds on Capitol Hill as the Senate prepares for confirmation hearings. U.S. Solicitor General Elena Kagan, by all accounts an outstanding legal mind, is being questioned by some for never having been a judge, and her conservative foes voice the complaint that she will not be a "strict constructionist" when it comes to interpreting the Constitution."

The very first problem here is calling Barack Hussein Obama "the president" which is about as ignorant as anyone can get seeing that he, Barack, an "avid constitutional lawyer", knowing what the USC says about the Natural Born status … well, you know where I'd go with that one, right?

And what about US Solicitor Elena Kagan and her "outstanding legal mind" not being a judge? What of that?

"On October 3, 2005, Harriet Miers was nominated for Associate Justice of the U.S. Supreme Court by President George W. Bush to replace retiring Associate Justice Sandra Day O'Connor. Miers was, at the time, White House Counsel, and had previously served in several roles both during Bush's tenure as Governor of Texas and President."

Well, oh phooey. What did the American Leftinistra say about her? "Supreme Court nominee bows out, cites Senate document grab." Well, now. They were going after the Bush Papers and that's why she bowed out. So what is Obama doing at this very moment? "White House: Obama may use executive privilege to withhold Kagan documents." Harrumph, even. I wonder where all that is in the illustrious newsies. And, I wonder what this Leftinistra hack daddy Bob Ray thinks of Harriet Miers. More than likely, seeing that he is a Leftinistra hack daddy, he was criticizing Miers just like some alleged Conservatives were.

If Elena Kagan was of a sound mind on a legal setting, why is Obama going to use an Executive Order to cease and desist Kagan's papers from coming out? Don't We The People have the right to know? Oh. Wait. We The People don't count. Just ask Bobbie Ray.

Just to let everyone know about the United States Supreme Court. No one has to be a Judge and Harriet Miers was a Judge but the Leftinistra hated her because President Bush nominated her and for no other reason. A Supreme Court Justice doesn't even need to be an attorney. A SCOTUS Justice, according to the Founding Fathers could be just a regular person - you know, one of those We The People that don't count anymore. But wait. The Founding Fathers were just rich old white men...just ask Bobbie Ray.

And what about being one of those "strict constructionist" types. Seeing that the Leftinistra can't hardly stand the United States Constitution because that very document puts the kibosh on every single Leftinistra hack's job performance, every single Justice now needs to be a Leftinistra hack daddy and a Marxist-sociopath. Right? A Supreme Court Justice, by the very nature of the United States Constitution of which they are all SWORN to defend and protect, are not allowed to be a Leftinistra, a Democrat, a Republican, an Independent, a Marxist-sociopath but someone that does not interpret the United States Constitution but applies the United States Constitution. Period. End of story. SO what else is new to this Leftinistra hack daddy Bobbie Ray?

"By "strict constructionist" the detractors mean someone who, in their opinion, will interpret our sacred Constitution just as the Founding Fathers "intended". Because you are going to hear a lot about that revered document in the coming weeks, I think it is important for us to note that just as the Founders were imperfect, so was that manuscript they produced and adopted as the foundation of our democratic republic."

Judas H Priest. Can you get any more unconstitutional than this? First of all, Bobbie Ray, we are a Constitutional Republic, a Federal Republic and not a democratic anything. Try and find in the USC where the term "democracy" is ever used. It won't take very long to find out. Benjamin Franklin told an elderly woman way back when that "they gave us a republic if you can keep it". This moosetwit has fallen hook line and sinker for the Marxist-sociopathic change up of our governmental philosophy. Pity that. He is apparently an over-educated idiot.

However, he almost got this part correct in tat the Founding Fathers were not perfect. Why? Because they are human beings. That's why they are not perfect. As for the rest of his convoluted disparities? Hogwash.

"That manuscript"? That manuscript? You mean the United States Constitution that can be changed by AMENDMENTS. Right? Idiot. That "manuscript" Bobbie Ray is in fact the Founding DOCUMENT of this great Nation and if you don't like it, move to the nearest Marxist-sociopathic Nation of your choice, pal.

"Revered document"? Not in your wet dreams bud. Bobbie Ray hates the Founding Documents of this Nation so the only thing revered here is its utter destruction and that is exactly what Obama is trying to do.

"I thought about this more as I heard a local radio

commentator railing against the late Supreme Court Justice Thurgood Marshall who, in a speech in 1987, was making this same point much more eloquently than I."

More eloquently than you, Bobbie Ray? Judas H Priest. How eloquent can a Marxist-sociopath be, especially tainting yourself with a Marxist-sociopathic nitwit like Thurgood Marshall? Man oh man could that guy rewrite history, couldn't he?

"When I reread that speech the other day, it occurred to me that every American — especially those senators who will sit in judgment of Kagan, a woman who once clerked for Marshall — ought to be familiar with what Marshall had to say during the 200th anniversary of the Constitution."

Oh good Lord. We are familiar with what the idiot Marxist-sociopath Marshall said and it couldn't be any more far from the Truth than you will ever be, Bobbie Ray. In essence this is what Thurgood Marshall had to say: everything in the United States Constitution is so bad and so wrong we need to rewrite all of our history and all of our laws and fashion ourselves with Black Liberation Theology and Karl Marx. He was nominated by LBJ one of the best Marxist-sociopaths that had ever crossed the line of Presidential tomfoolery outside of Barack Hussein Obama. But, get a load of this crap...

""To the contrary, the government they devised was defective from the start, requiring several amendments, a civil war and momentous social transformation to attain the system of constitutional government and its respect for the individual freedoms and human rights we hold as fundamental today. When contemporary Americans cite 'The Constitution,' they invoke a concept that is vastly different from what the Framers barely began to construct two centuries ago". Sound arrogant? Bold? Out-of-touch? Un-American? Well, Marshall explained that the first three words in the preamble to the document, "We the people," did not include the majority of Americans. It specifically stated that it applied to "the whole Number of free Persons." But on the basic right to vote, he pointed out, the Framers excluded Negro slaves, although they were counted for the purpose of congressional representation (at three-fifths), and it would be 135 years before women gained that right."

Thurgood Marshall. Karl Marx must have laughing his arse off over this idiot.

Social transformation - sound familiar? What does Obama call it? Read it for yourself: Everything I Have Written On The Übermessias Obama. Of everything that idiot stated or will state in the future, he reeks of Marxist-sociopathic stupidity. However, Marshall and this gasbag Bobbie Ray do say something that some today are just finding out - they do not know the United State Constitution because no one teaches it any more. They teach precedent law and case law. That's it. And that is changing. More and more people are getting into the United States Constitution and that is why men and women are losing in their primaries across this Nation and that's a good thing.

And yes, Marshall was an un-American as much as an un-American can get. And no, he wasn't arrogant at all. He was just too stupid to understand the USC that he swore to defend and protect. Funny how all these people that are sworn to defend and protect something never do. I suppose that is merely one of those moments of fluff these days.

Marshall's ramblings of We The People - something the

Marxist sociopaths hate with a passion - is nothing but a lot of ignorance seeing that he swore to defend and protect the United States Constitution and if he did mean what he said, he needed to be impeached from his office as most of them now, today. We The People means exactly what it says it means - We The People. Our Constitution was written for We The People and the Constitution can be changed - and it has been changed - by the Amendments processes, and not for We The Congress or We The Judiciary or We The Leaders or We The Ignorant Pompous Nitwits of the Media.

Oh. But wait. Bobbie Ray and Thurgood Marshall are members of the Black Clans so the Amendments that took place don't mean anything to these maroons do they? They never happened and they are all slaves now. I see. My bad. Moron.

"In 1857, the infamous Dred Scott decision by the Supreme Court declared black people "property" and "beings of an inferior order, and altogether unfit to associate with the white race...; and so far inferior, that they had no rights which the white man was bound to respect ...."Referring to that writing by Chief Justice Roger Taney, Marshall said, "And, so, nearly seven decades after the Constitutional Convention, the Supreme Court reaffirmed the prevailing opinion of the Framers regarding the rights of Negroes in America. It took a bloody civil war before the 13th Amendment could be adopted to abolish slavery, though not the consequences slavery would have for future Americans."

I won't get into all of that because none of it means a damned thing. The Civil War wasn't fought over the Slaves. It was fought over States Rights. Do some homework, Bobbie Ray. Your stupidity is "Rather" evident. Leave all that nonsense with Al Sharpton and Jesse Jackson.

The next few paragraphs deal with the utter destruction of his own race and I'll let him simmer on that one. The last part is what has floored me and floored me good. Listen/read this…

"Marshall concluded his remarks by saying, "I plan to celebrate the bicentennial of the Constitution as a living document, including the Bill of Rights and the other amendments protecting individual freedoms and human rights." In addition to drafting and adopting the Constitution, the next best thing that the Framers did was to provide a mechanism to change it. We should keep this in mind always, but especially as we move forward with confirming a new Supreme Court justice."

The United States Constitution is a Living and Breathing Document but that's because of the Amendments Processes and not some nitwit on SCOTUS that makes laws at will. But that's not the flooring matter here. This dingbat has stated time and time again how stupid the Framers were but here and now he states that those idiots made it possible to change the USC by Amendments. And yes, Bobbie Ray, we should keep that in mind always but actually do it…change the USC by Amendments and not what some joker in the judiciary says we should do.

Nitwit. For all the rest of the items I didn't cover in this article, one needs to go there and read all about it in a various number of articles. The Marxist-sociopaths are wringing their hands and I know it. And so do they.

Was I harsh and mean spirited? I sure hope so. The time for talking nice-nice is over and done with.

So, our Constitution was not set in stone, then. Can you believe this trivial tripe? In the Scripture, while we are talking about "stones", there 389 verses of Scripture which talk about stones and various other topics along the lines of stones.

Many things are set in stone in Scripture, as in His Holy Word, and seeing that God gave us this Constitution, wouldn't it have been prudent if our Constitution was in fact set into stone, by God Himself? Can we not amend our Law of The Land by changing our Law of The Land via the very Constitution itself – as it prescribes to do?

I find this article by this man of trivia to be equivalent to a demon and keeping things simple, just like our Constitution, and our Bibles, makes life so much easier, doesn't it?

I find it also accepting man's ideas over God's ideas. It is also an amazing thing, at least to myself, that when the Scriptures are taken out of context, these same people do the same thing to our Law of The Land, our Constitution.

Matthew 15:9; "But in vain they do worship me, teaching for doctrines the commandments of men."

Mark 7:7; "Howbeit in vain do they worship me, teaching for doctrines the commandments of men."

Titus 1:14; "Not giving heed to Jewish fables, and commandments of men, that turn from the truth."

Matthew 5:19; "Whosoever therefore shall break one of these least commandments, and shall teach men so, he shall be called the least in the kingdom of heaven: but whosoever shall do and teach them, the same shall be called great in the kingdom of heaven."

Colossians 2:22; "Which all are to perish with the using;) after the commandments and doctrines of man."

The Scriptures are truly a wondrous thing aren't they?

Chapter 4: Good vs Evil...It Is Your Choice[20]

Where is this Nation we call America going? Where are the minority in numbers taking us? Let's face it. Around 25% of this Nation's citizenry are flat out cold-hearted Marxist-sociopaths. Is that a good thing or is that a bad thing? Also remember that in our very foundation it was what is now called the conservatives that started this Nation called America and their numbers were very few. However, the Nation survived that war against Common Law, which makes me wonder why people of today declare that we are founded on Common Law. We fought Common Law. We defeated it. What we are founded on is the Law of Nations and I am not talking about the organization, which came before the United Nations either. So, where are we going?

Our Nation, today, in the 21st century, is being torn apart by Good vs Evil with that Good vs Evil not conducive to any political party. We are not talking about Liberal vs Conservative. We are not talking about Republican vs Democrat. We are not talking about any MO of Independent either. We are talking Good vs Evil and that is God vs Satan. It's that simple. Are we, as a Nation, on God's side or are we on Satan's side. It is your choice as an individual to choose and not some morphed collective thought pattern.

And then, there is always Obama. He is singularly the most corrupted community organizer on this side of Hell and quite possibly on the other side. The soon to be Club Gitmo detainees to come to the United States is for what reason? It is Good vs Evil. There are many elements involved for their detention at Club Gitmo but these particular detainees have been slated to come to New York City for what reason?

Dan Riehl writes: "Let's just hope he isn't successful in dragging America too far down with him before he's run out of town in 2012 as the absolutely worst chief executive in America's modern history. With his latest stupid move he's simply handing radical Islam a perfect propaganda tool and causing NYC and America to experience more sadness and potential mayhem than they've already endured due to those miscreants."

Is this Good vs Evil? Is this Liberal vs Conservative? Is this any political party vs any other political party? I'm calling it Good vs Evil because that is exactly what it is…Good vs Evil, no matter how anyone tries to spin this incident. Why place the country and of all places, NYC, in such a turmoil when the vast majority of Americans are dead-set against this and especially the people of NYC? In hearing after hearing of this, Eric Holder was shown to be a complete fool and then Obama said, "I didn't say we could do this." It is Good vs Evil, plain and simple. The Evil One, Obama, has spoken. And that's just the way a failed community organizer does. Nothing.

Obama is a disgrace to any Freedom Loving man or woman. Or toad. Or butterfly. Or any other creature. He is a disgrace and the worst community organizer in the entire world. Pacific President? Not hardly. Just look at the laughs he received from everyone over there! Bowing? Please.

Obama lacks wisdom. He lacks Patriotism and I mean genuine Patriotism and not some odd, bizarre and morphed Patriotism. His such a lack of Patriotism to this degree hides the fact that he is a disgrace. An incompetent disgrace at that. I hear others saying things like; "Oh, he was just trying to do....yaddayaddayadda" I' m sick of it all and it is Good vs Evil. Obama is Evil. He is not the anti-Christ but he must be in the short-run for it.

Since Obama's coronation, pretty much half of our Nation America has come to despise The Evil One and hopefully, hopefully, people will come to their senses and evict this upstart community organizer and send him out on a rail, tarred and feathered as was done in the Good Old Days. His Evil, dumb and pathetic Holier Than Thou stupidity will get him thrown out of the now known as Marxist House so far away that he'll wind up in the Marxist-sociopathic Nation of his choice, and it will not be America. We could send him to Europe but Europe is currently swinging towards conservatism because their Marxist-sociopathic life styles are not working. Just look what the Jihad is doing to them all.

Who knows? Perhaps a third-world no-place will take him in. What or where else would take his lamed community organizing skill set? Obama is our stain on logic and proper placement. He ran on Hope and Change but where is it? Obama is Bush III and GWB was a Globalist. What's the difference? At least GWB was good on the War, to a point. Obama? No such luck.

Obama was the best the Democrats could even hope to aspire to? Please. And the Republicans? Please. Their answer was John McCain? When did that ever stand a chance? Sarah Palin kept John McCain from being the first Republican Walter Mondale and the idiot Democrat Bob Beckel? He lead the worse campaign in this Nation's history so who is he to speak out for The Evil One Obama? Is he kidding me? Bob Beckel. Another Evil for this Nation that was Founded upon the Godly principles of which our very documents proclaim. It is Good vs Evil and Obama is the Evil One.

It is very much time to turn every Congress Critter out on their ears and if there are enough good ones, later on, they'll be back. We need to start all over under the Constitution of the United States because currently we have a Congress that does not hold any correlation to the United States Constitution and have used men and women that wear their black pajamas to court to make administrative ideas and make laws. Show me in the USC where that is and I'll abide by it. It is Good vs Evil and I choose Good.

The Debonair Dude once said, recently; "Is our president plain stupid, or he has maliciously set up the freeing of those terrorists? Rights? What rights? Why are these terrorists being given the same rights as Americans? They are not Americans, they are terrorists put them in front of a military tribunal. One has to only wonder if we will also read him his Miranda rights? Are we to believe that the man who freed the FALN, and 2 weather underground terrorists, is somehow not going to set these vermin free, and this is somehow not a plan to do just that?"

Ladies and gentlemen? That is The Evil One. Take it or leave it.

Good versus Evil. Which one will you take?

Hebrews 5:14; "But strong meat belongeth to them that are of full age, even those who by reason of use have their senses exercised to discern both good and evil."

Which "meat" do you eat?

Psalm 52:3; "Thou lovest evil more than good; and lying rather than to speak righteousness. Selah."

Proverbs 14:22; "Do they not err that devise evil? but mercy and truth shall be to them that devise good."

Proverbs 15:3; "The eyes of the LORD are in every place, beholding the evil and the good."

Isaiah 5:20; "Woe unto them that call evil good, and good evil; that put darkness for light, and light for darkness; that put bitter for sweet, and sweet for bitter!"

Jeremiah 4:22; "For my people is foolish, they have not known me; they are sottish children, and they have none understanding: they are wise to do evil, but to do good they have no knowledge."

Romans 3:8; "And not rather, (as we be slanderously reported, and as some affirm that we say,) Let us do evil, that good may come? whose damnation is just."

1 Peter 3:11; "Let him eschew evil, and do good; let him seek peace, and ensue it."

Chapter 5: Do Birthers Rock and Roll or Stop and Drool?[7]

The Snooper Report has written many articles on Barack Hussein Obama's birth certificate, the United States Constitution and Obama's natural-born status and what all of it means. I don't care if Obama spent some time in Indonesia. I don't care if Obama was born on an Atoll in the middle of East Bedidguwits on a stormy or a sunny day. I don't even care if he was born in Hawaii. None of that means anything to me. What I do care about is the United States Constitution. Period.

Some people will comment on this article as if they do know something about the United States Constitution and will tell me that Common Law says this that or the other and that doesn't fly with me because "case law" and "precedent law" means nothing to me because both are contrary to the United States Constitution. Period.

Some people will comment on this article as if they do know

something about the United States Constitution and will tell me that "natural-born" equates to being born in the United States, which is exactly the opposite of what it really means.

Some people will comment on this article as if they do know something about something and will say all manner of silligisms that mean absolutely nothing when compared to the United States Constitution. So, before you all make a comment which will get you called all those "evil names", just shut up and go away.

So, do you know the United States Constitution? Does Confederate Yankee? Does Hot Air? Does Michelle Malkin? Do the Senators know the USC? Does anyone in the House know the USC? No, they do not. Does Obama know the USC? No, he doesn't unless it doesn't go far enough. Now the Confederate Yankee, Hot Air and Michelle Malkin and a host of other "conservatives" haven't taken the Oath of Service but the Senators, House Members and the alleged "president" have taken the Oath and have lied their rear ends off just to call themselves what they call themselves - YOUR Leaders. They aren't "leaders". They are "servants". End of that story.

Let us begin here. In the original Constitution capitalized letters mean something. In today's Constitution, in those little pocket type units, capitalized letters are gone. I always thought that was OK and then I learned later on that all that is OK if the reader knows what the original has stated before. The original Constitution currently "lives" in a vacuum box, sealed from the elements and cannot breath so the "living and breathing" document as some people call the Constitution cannot live or breath. The only life and breath of the USC is if one Amends the document which is Constitutional.

In Article 1, Section 8, where the "laws of what the Congress is Constitutionally obligated to do", we read the following...(capital letters emboldened by me)

"To define and punish Piracies and Felonies committed on the high Seas, and Offences against the Law of Nations;"

What do the capitalized letters mean or is it just some bunch of old white men making no sense? If you must, you can read all about it in Madison's notes but the obvious even to the oblivious will know that capitalized letters do in fact mean something.

In today's Constitution, the kind one would place in their pockets, Article 1, Section 8 reads this way:

"To define and punish Piracies and Felonies committed on the high Seas, and Offences against the law of nations;"

Now, unless you are reading the Heritage Foundations little pocket guide, why in the world would Law of Nations not be capitalized? Why? This is because that whoever decided to turn the United States Constitution into some morphed identity of dumb or because the ones doing the deed didn't know what a capitalized letter meant, the document that most people have will not have Law of Nations capitalized. Ever. So, what does the Law of Nations mean? It means quite a bit.

The Founding Fathers were very smart and highly educated. Did they know how to get to the moon? No but that doesn't matter, does it? They spoke many languages and were well versed in the governments of the day and they were also concerned about the New Government about to begin and where it was going to go. They also had three books called the Law of Nations written by Vattel, a Frenchman. Out of many items in the volumes, this is said about "natural-born" citizenship...

This citation below is From Jadem in an article here: The Tenuous and Effervescent Obama Birth Certificate

"t/The Law of Nations
Book 1, Chap 19, § 212. Citizens and natives.
The citizens are the members of the civil society; bound to this society by certain duties, and subject to its authority, they equally participate in its advantages. The natives, or natural-born citizens, are those born in the country, of parents who are citizens. As the society cannot exist and perpetuate itself otherwise than by the children of the citizens, those children naturally follow the condition of their fathers, and succeed to all their rights..."

First edition was in 1759. And how could Ben Franklin have thanked Charles W.F. Dumas for giving him a translation of the Law of Nations in 1775? Stating in his thank you letter:

"I am much obliged by the kind present you have made us of your edition of Vattel. It came to us in good season, when the circumstances of a rising state make it necessary frequently to consult the law of nations. Accordingly, that copy which I kept, has been continually in the hands of the members of our congress, now sitting..."

"Also other Founders of the U.S. also quoted and referred to Vattel many times over before the Constitution was drafted. Which means either they could read it in the original language, or it was translated before the time that you state."

Jadem was answering the usual libtard that either hates the United States Constitution or is definitely unread in it. Some will get upset that I said that but, that's just the way it is. Educate yourself in the United States Constitution because that is all we have. Our Congress Critters hate the document so badly that they use the SCOTUS and other federal judges to circumvent the document and to legislate around the document, which by the way, is unconstitutional to do so. That is in the Constitution that they all swear to uphold, defend and protect. Kind of odd, isn't it? I swore the Oath years ago and it stands with me now, today, and forever.

As I have said before, I am a Birther but I suppose that I am not. I don't care where, when or who Obama was born. All I care about is if Obama has two American citizens and if he does have two American citizens as parents, than Obama is a "natural-born" citizen. Don't know if this is true? Read Madison's notes on the Constitution[9,10].

As far as I can tell, Obama is not a natural-born American citizen and this is why Obama has not presented his birth certificate for all to see. It is theoretically locked up some place in Hawaii unseen by anyone except libtards that have said they saw it...after it was locked up. Hot Air says so. Confederate Yankee says so. Michelle Malkin says so. Why? They think the issue is closed and it is not closed. It is only closed when one is too afraid to ask the Truth.

If Obama has two American parents, he passes muster. Until he shows it, the birth certificate, he is an unknown and could have proved it when he himself was in on McCain's "issue".

I have written on this subject like I have so stated:

See these posts: I'M A BIRTHER! - Does The Illegal Alien Barack Have A Birth Certificate? (is Barack an illegal alien? no one knows) - The Ever Evasive and Mysterious Soetoro Birth Certificate - The Obama AWOL Birth Certificate Update - Birth Certificate The Illegal Alien's (Barack Obama) AWOL - Can We See Soetoro's Birth Certificate Yet? –

...and I would like to add this section about McCain v Obama...

"He could have very well ended all discussions of his natural-born status when John McCain's was ended but he did not. Perhaps because he could not and cannot still.

In April of 2008, Senator McCain's "natural born" citizen status was settled by Senate Resolution 511. I thought it peculiar that Patrick Leahy would make the comment that the term "natural born citizen" was not defined in the Constitution when it clearly is defined. One doesn't need to be a rocket scientist to detect the Constitutional definition when the definition is clearly stated in the Constitution. There is other verbiage in the Resolution that is equally suspect.

"Whereas previous presidential candidates were born outside of the United States of America and were understood to be eligible to be President;"

This statement was added to the Resolution by none other than Barack Hussein Obama. Why?

"In the process of my self-admonitions of following for a well crafted scam, I ran across this post recently after Pamela Geller rocked my world back in July.

"From Obama own website:
Since Sen. Obama has neither renounced his U.S. citizenship nor sworn an oath of allegiance to Kenya, his Kenyan citizenship automatically expired on Aug. 4,1982."

Question?

How could it expire, if he never had it? [END]

Indeed. My learning and my cravings for knowledge will never end on this subject. In the linked post, I learned several other items of interest and I do believe that honest people will also see the light, as it were. Naturally, the apologists that can never admit to being in error will claim high and mighty blissful ignorance."

There's more...

"During the campaign for either the presidency of the United States on one side of the aisle and the campaign for the First Czar of the Disunited Soviet Socialist States of KKK-A on the other side of the aisle, the topic of natural-born status for Obama arose and the Obama Goon Squads rose to the occasion. What did they do? They questioned McCain's natural-born status.

What did McCain do? He produced his papers and what came of it? In April of 2008, Senator McCain's "natural born" citizen status was settled by Senate Resolution 511. Soon thereafter, the cowards of the GOP did not press Obama to produce his papers and accused everyone that questioned Obama's natural-born status as racists or other inane name-calling.

Why wasn't there a Senate Resolution for Obama? Why

does he get a free pass? Obama, does not meet the Constitutional requirements, that's why. Until the Imam of Obama proves his bona fides, he is the Usurper, the Liar in Chief and the Fraud in Chief and I will not recognize his authority or the authority of his illegal and unconstitutional administration, comprised of lobbyists Obama said he wouldn't have, tax cheats, crooks and liars. I will also not recognize the authority of the United States Congress whether it be the House of Unconstitutional Unrepresentatives or the Unconstitutional Senate that has unconstitutionally confirmed unconstitutional secretaries of the Interior and State."

So, Obama, where is the birth certificate? I know he has one. And I know he can show it. And I know that he will not because he doesn't have TWO American citizens as parents. Period. End of discussion.

Media Liberals Paint Conservatives as 'Birthers', But First Birthers Were Dems

"Here's something you won't hear from the liberal media: that whole "birther" conspiracy movement? Yeah, that was started by a couple of Democrats, and neither is named Orly Taitz."

From The Federalist Blog - "The common law of England is not the common law of these States." —George Mason

What might the phrase "natural-born citizen" of the United States imply under the U.S. Constitution? The phrase has always been obscure due to the lack of any single authoritative source to confer in order to understand the condition of citizenship the phrase recognizes. Learning what the phrase might have meant following the Declaration of Independence, and the adoption of the Fourteenth Amendment, requires detective work. As with all detective work, eliminating the usual suspects from the beginning goes a long way in quickly solving a case.

What Natural-Born Citizen Could Not Mean

Could a natural-born citizen simply mean citizenship due to place of birth?

Unlikely in the strict sense because we know one can be native born and yet not a native born citizen of this country. There were even disputes whether anyone born within the District of Columbia or in the territories were born citizens of the United States (they were generally referred to as "inhabitants" instead.) National Government could make no "territorial allegiance" demands within the several States because as Madison explained it, the "powers reserved to the several States will extend to all the objects which, in the ordinary course of affairs, concern the lives, liberties, and properties of the people, and the internal order, improvement, and prosperity of the State."

Jurisdiction over citizenship via birth within the several States was part of the "ordinary course of affairs" of the States that only local laws could affect. Early acts of Naturalization recognized the individual State Legislatures as the only authority who could make anyone a citizen of a State. Framer James Wilson said, "a citizen of the United States is he, who is a citizen of at least some one state in the Union." These citizens of each State were united together through Article IV, Sec. II of the U.S. Constitution, and thus, no act of Congress was required to make citizens of the individual States citizens of the United States.

Prior to the Revolutionary War place of birth within the dominions of the crown was the principle criterion for establishing perpetual allegiance and citizenship. After independence each State was free to establish their own maxims on the subject. James Madison's own State of Virginia adopted a birthright law authored by Thomas Jefferson in 1779 that recognized parentage (citizenship of father) in determining citizenship of the child:

[A]ll infants, wheresoever born, whose father, if living, or otherwise, whose mother was a citizen at the time of their birth, or who migrate hither, their father, if living, or otherwise, their mother becoming a citizen, or who migrate hither without father or mother, shall be deemed citizens of this Commonwealth until they relinquish that character, in manner as hereinafter expressed; and all others not being citizens of any, of the United States of America, shall be deemed aliens.

Some States made citizenship conditional on either parent in terms of their citizenship, such as Kentucky: "[E]very child, wherever born, whose father or mother was or shall be a citizen of Kentucky at the birth of such child, shall be deemed citizens of that State." One common law found in a number of States that defined those born as citizens read, "All persons born in this state, and resident within it, except the children of transient aliens, and of alien public ministers and consuls, etc."

From Jadem via DM and text:

Another good article to add: The Natural Born Citizen Clause of Our U.S. Constitution Requires that Both of the Child's Parents Be U.S. Citizens At the Time of Birth

Just in case "someone" wants to discuss "court cases", here you go. I have the first two paragraphs of the entire article here: (I removed an original text as a link and placed it into the Scalia verbiage)

"When interpreting the Constitution, we must decide whether we will look to the document as an original and static one whose meaning has already been established at a given time by the People and its Framers or one that is living and which can be changed over any given time by a court of law. See the address of Justice Antonin Scalia to the 2008 Annual National Lawyers Convention on November 22, 2008, at the Mayflower Hotel, in Washington, D.C. (advocates originalism rather than living constitutionalism). I submit that Article II's "natural born Citizen" clause has a fixed and knowable meaning which was established at the time of its drafting and should therefore be interpreted through the eyes of the original Framers that drafted and ratified the clause so as to determine what they intended the clause to mean (original intent theory). I also submit that we should interpret the "natural born Citizen" clause in a way that reasonable persons living at the time of its adoption would have declared the ordinary meaning of the text to be (original meaning theory). This is not living constitutionalism but rather originalism or textualism as applied to interpreting the Constitution. It is this latter approach that I will utilize in this article.

E. Vattel stated in 1758, as translated into English in 1797 : "The citizens are the members of the civil society: bound to this society by certain duties, and subject to its authority, they equally participate in its advantages. The natives, or natural-born citizens, are those born in the country, of parents who are citizens. As the society cannot exist and perpetuate itself otherwise than by the children of the

49

citizens, those children naturally follow the condition of their fathers, and succeed to all their rights. The society is supposed to desire this, in consequence of what it owes to its own preservation; and it is presumed, as matter of course, that each citizen, on entering into society, reserves to his children the right of becoming members of it. The country of the fathers is therefore that of the children; and these become true citizens merely by their tacit consent. We shall soon see, whether, on their coming to the years of discretion, they may renounce their right, and what they owe to the society in which they were born. I say, that, in order to be of the country, it is necessary that a person be born of a father who is a citizen; for if he is born there of a foreigner, it will be only the place of his birth, and not his country." E. Vattel, The Law of Nations or Principles of Natural Law, Sec. 212 Citizens and natives. In Footnote 1 at the end of Sec. 212, Vattel stated that "as a general rule" the child inherits his father's citizenship, or his mother's but only if she is not married."

Many people cannot believe that Obama has no American daddy but as I have said from the very beginning of this Obama unconstitutional "rezident", he ain't no natural born anything but a damned natural born LIAR.

From Jadem: The REAL birther question

"Dan Riehl, the GOP apologist, perhaps a "conservative" but I doubt it has this to say: Oh Geez: Fifty Percent Of AZ Legislature Are Birthers - that right there strikes a blow against his credibility about anything and living too close to DC has rattled his brain cells.

He doesn't know about Vattel's Law of Nations. Why? Because he doesn't know the US Constitution like he says he does."

All people want to do is to have someone prove they are natural-born because the unconstitutional SCOTUS will not. Just look what happened to the Governor of Michigan now...she has dual citizenship so she is now qualified to be POTUS? I wonder how Dan would react to that.

For anyone that knows to do good but doesn't do that which is good, is abhorrent to God. Well, that's what the Scriptures so state. **James 4:17**; "Therefore to him that knoweth to do good, and doeth it not, to him it is sin." What is Obama and his unconstitutional allies waiting for? Oh. Never mind.

Isn't Obama a "christian"? **3 John 1:11**; "Beloved, follow not that which is evil, but that which is good. He that doeth good is of God: but he that doeth evil hath not seen God." I think not.

Chapter 6: We Didn't Start This War[8]

Mike Allen / The Politico: Obama to address nation next week

"President Obama is expected to announce his Afghanistan policy with an address to the nation next Tuesday, Dec. 1, likely in prime time, officials told POLITICO. — Obama held his ninth formal Afghanistan strategy session in the Situation Room on Monday night."

McClatchy Washington Bureau: Obama plans to send 34,000 more troops to Afghanistan

"WASHINGTON — President Barack Obama met Monday evening with his national security team to finalize a plan to dispatch some 34,000 additional U.S. troops over the next year to what he's called "a war of necessity" in Afghanistan, U.S. officials told McClatchy."

McClatchy offers the most ignorant of ignorant things to deal with. Read that article and you just let me know. OK?

Who in the hell are we fighting? We are fighting a Global Jihad bent on the destruction of everything "western". They want and demand a Caliphate. That's their goal and due process of life and death. It is in their gene pools. Now, we have Jihadis in Minnesota running off to Somalia.

Feds charge 20 "young Americans" with joining Al-Qaeda-linked Somali jihad group

That is al Qaida in America ladies and gentlemen and I don't give a damn about any libtard moron that says any different. al Qaida is in the USA and they have been here for decades. I fought my first one here in 1971. That's a long time ago.

Who are we fighting in Afghanistan & Pakistan?

That's easy. It is the Global Jihad.

"The Warrior Legacy Institute announces the release of it's third paper "Who are we fighting in Afghanistan & Pakistan?" as well as an accompanying video. This complements the previous papers and videos on "A Population-Centric Counterinsurgency Primer" and "Counterterror as Strategy for the Af/Pak Theater". All of these are written so they can be understood by and educate all Americans regardless of their knowledge about military topics. Our hope is that this will allow them to follow the debate about this vital subject from an informed perspective."

We didn't start this war. We have it pretty much finished in Iraq. Now, Obama wants us to lose in Afghanistan that was once upon a time the war to fight if there ever was a war, according to The Obama. Obama? Liar. Get over it. You elected the moron and you can have the bastard. Keep him in your closet for a nice rainy day.

Nothing like backing yourself into a corner. Right? As far as many that know me know this. Many times I have said that the Defeatocrats are backing themselves into a hole claiming that the Republicans did it. Obama cannot lay that one out this time.

Obama To Hold Another Prime Timer To Explain Our Afghanistan Strategy To Islamic Extremists

Obama is waiting until next Tuesday when "V" is on, that tramples The One's subject matter, to deliver a Nation Wide Obamagang tripper.

"Holding off till Tuesday also apparently will allow Obama to get in touch with Democrat leaders and his unhinged ObamaZombie base to explain why he would send more troops. They all knew his campaign promise was a lie, but, he kinda backed himself into a corner."

Get out of that corner.

Obama's decision: 34,000 troops to Afghanistan

A far cry from the 60,000 General McChrystal said he needed to win the damn war, eh, Czarboe?

So, Czarboe is sending 34,000 to the areas where he isn't giving Afghanistan land to who?

Full-throttle appeasement: US offers Taliban control of five provinces in return for halt to missile attacks

"Maybe Obama is hoping that those chimerical "moderate Taliban" of whom he is so fond will end up running these provinces, and give up their desire to win the rest. "Afghan Source: The U.S. Has Offered the Taliban Control in Return for Quiet," from MEMRI, November 22:"

Go read that one, again. I know I keep telling you all about this but someone needs to understand that Obama is in fact a Jihadi clown.

Amid Growing Pressure, Obama to Back McChrystal's Troops Surge in Afghanistan

No he isn't. 34,000 Troops is NOT the 60,000 Troops requested.

Obama hates this Nation. Obama hates Conservatives and any other alleged and pretend "moderate". He hates the US Military because the military is in the way. So, I hate Obama and I sure do hope that this quack of an illegal rezident gets impeached soon enough.

Many years ago, the United States entered into a war between the Islami's of the Barbary Coast and they were defeated handsomely but at a cost, as most wars will cost. Here is just a small bit about this war - "When Jefferson became president in 1801 he refused to accede to Tripoli's demands for an immediate payment of $225,000 and an annual payment of $25,000. **The pasha of Tripoli then declared war on the United States**. Although as secretary of state and vice president he had opposed developing an American navy capable of anything more than coastal defense, President Jefferson dispatched a squadron of naval vessels to the Mediterranean. As he declared in his first annual message to Congress: "To this state of general peace with which we have been blessed, one only exception exists. Tripoli, the least considerable of the Barbary States, had come forward with demands unfounded either in right or in compact, and had permitted itself to denounce war, on our failure to comply before a given day. The style of the demand admitted but one answer. I sent a small squadron of frigates into the Mediterranean..."

The American show of force quickly awed Tunis and Algiers into breaking their alliance with Tripoli. The humiliating loss of the frigate Philadelphia and the capture of her captain and crew in Tripoli in 1803, criticism from his political opponents, and even opposition within his own cabinet did not deter Jefferson from his chosen course during four years of war. The aggressive action of Commodore Edward Preble (1803-4) forced Morocco out of the fight and his five bombardments of Tripoli restored some order to the Mediterranean. However, it was not until 1805, when an American fleet under Commodore John Rogers and a land force raised by an American naval agent to the Barbary powers, Captain William Eaton, threatened to capture Tripoli and install the brother of Tripoli's pasha on the throne, that a treaty brought an end to the hostilities. Negotiated by Tobias Lear, former secretary to President Washington and now consul general in Algiers, the treaty of 1805 still required the United States to pay a ransom of $60,000 for each of the sailors held by the day of Algiers, and so it went without Senatorial consent until April 1806. Nevertheless, Jefferson was able to report in his sixth annual message to Congress in December 1806 that in addition to the successful completion of the Lewis and Clark expedition, "The states on the coast of Barbary seem generally disposed at present to respect our peace and friendship[11].""

So, here we have a man, saying that term loosely, Obama, filling in a position of which he has no authority to be in, acting as the Jihadi that he is, trying to destroy this nation through the military of which he hates so much.

So, no, we did not start this war at all. We are in the middle of this war that started long before Thomas Jefferson became our President. So much for the history lesson(s).

Matthew 24:6; "And ye shall hear of wars and rumours of wars: see that ye be not troubled: for all these things must come to pass, but the end is not yet."

Mark 13:7; "And when ye shall hear of wars and rumours of wars, be ye not troubled: for such things must needs be; but the end shall not be yet."

Seeing that there is a war between God and Satan, no matter where you stand within the cancer of political correctness, multiculturalism and identity politics, there will be human wars upon human wars until such a time that the Son of Man will return to reign upon this earth. Then and only then will we have peace on this planet.

The myth of global warming will not kill us…only Satan can kill us if God allows him to, and that is the end of that discussion.

Chapter 7 - Democrats and Terrorists and now the Republicans; what's the difference and what we do about it$_{12,13}$?

Have you ever noticed that the verbiage regurgitated by either the Democrat Party leadership and those nice religious people are, far the most part, identical? I have approximately 340 articles on this subject should you care to check them out.

At Gateway Pundit, there is an article about how the Taliban are going to take care of their journalists if they don't shape up and quit lying. After I read the article, I detected the very familiar rhetoric offered up by the American Moonbat and those that cater and pander to that crowd for the express purpose to gain political power and gain.

Journalists Told to Quit Lying Or Face a Whipping ... sound familiar?

From Donald Douglas: Taliban Propaganda Channel on

YouTube: Mujahideen Islamic Emirate of Afghanistan, Jihad Against American Puppets, Zionist Intruders

The article is filled with links so go read the entire article. The problem I am having is with the liberal v terrorist actions. One cannot tell the difference between what a terrorist is talking about and what our own liberals are talking about. More often than not, one can hardly tell which one started and which one ended.

"But you know, of course, leftists will say it's all an American neo-imperialist campaign. We have no interests in Afghanistan. Bring the troops home. We can "invest" in pent up demands domestically. Hey, how about imposing a war "surtax"! That'll teach those pesky warmongers!

Sure, no problem, while we're at it we can turn a blind eye to the totalitarianism sweeping the barbaric periphery. But at least the Obama administration's on the job! These people deserve civilian trials:"

Civilian trials. And that is the numbnut way of looking at things. And, no, Donald Douglas is not the numbnut...the libtard/terrorists are. So, trying to determine what the differences are between the Marxist-sociopathic mentality and those mentalities of the Islamofascists is very difficult. Primarily, they both despise our Constitution and we can tell by their very verbiage they so aspire to shove down anyone else's throats. It is either do as we say or buzz off. Sounds kind of like that they have free speech and no one else does. Isn't that one of the tenets of our Constitution? Free Speech? To me, it seems like the liberals and the terrorists are more concerned about being offended by anything they don't like but I cannot find that in the Constitution. Anywhere. You?

A while back I wrote an article about the political aspects of life in general: Redefining The Center or the Moderate, written in May of 2009.

"If I have said this once, I have said it thousands of times. The Cultural Marxists, the proponents of political correctness, multiculturalism, diversity and identity politics have been rewriting and revising political science since I have been watching, studying and analyzing American politics. And, my tenure of paying attention spans 41 years. I have been paying attention to the political arena in this nation longer than most have served in DC. I have seen them all come and go. From that experience and not having been polluted by the captured audience mentality found in every place of education indoctrination in this nation, I have successfully adhered to the United States Constitution...for most of those years. I goofed up once and voted for Jimmy Carter."

Jimmy Carter. Thinking about The Obama and the liberals, aka ACORN, I have come to the conclusion that Jimmy Carter is way more substantial than the community organizer will ever be. And that isn't saying too much because it is Jimmy Carter why we have the Middle East as it is now. Go read that entire article complete with graphs. The problem? The political spectrum is no longer a circle and when you draw the circle, the far left and the far right are damn near identical. Scary. The linear graphs show them light years apart but they are not.

There are no differences between the American "liberal" - the Marxist-sociopaths - and the terrorists we are at war with. Name me one Pro American that has given money to the enemy. You won't find any but I can give you names of the plethora of "liberals" that do and will give more and more.

Now, in today's world in America, we can count on the current crop of Republicans in the same boat as the Democrats.

As in other books that I have written and on many radio shows that I have been on, the current crop of politicians in this country of America remind me of the Pharisees and the Sadducees.

Matthew 3:7; "But when he saw many of the Pharisees and Sadducees come to his baptism, he said unto them, O generation of vipers, who hath warned you to flee from the wrath to come?"

Matthew 16:6; "Then Jesus said unto them, Take heed and beware of the leaven of the Pharisees and of the Sadducees."

Matthew 16:11,12; "How is it that ye do not understand that I spake it not to you concerning bread, that ye should beware of the leaven of the Pharisees and of the Sadducees? Then understood they how that he bade them not beware of the leaven of bread, but of the doctrine of the Pharisees and of the Sadducees.

What do we do about it? Pray and then act upon your answers.

Chapter 8 - When Satan has beguiled the ignorant or, when liberal Christians think they know not so much[14]

I placed a picture of Obama up on Facebook and I degraded him much like he degrades everybody else but the libtards don't think these things through. Especially when the libtards live in Canada and have neither rhyme nor reason to get involved in American politics.

A person known as "Leila" on Facebook, if that is her real name (or it could be a man pretending to be a woman on Facebook (you never know these things), had and issue with the picture because "she has a picture up on her wall" of Obama and she decided that "as Christians we should pray for our leaders" and she raised the proverbial libtard reply like, how dare you talk bad about Obama because "he is the Anointed of God" for the Nation of America.

Now, Leila says she is from Canada but in her effervescent

demeanor, that changed, and her realm in Canada "is just a temporary thing" and that "she is coming back to America". I have heard all of this before but it doesn't change anything.

During the coarse of the conversation, Leila lied several times and when I called her on it she said that "she would not be called a liar" which made the comments about her from me make her into the liar that she is. Conversations with libtards is "Rather" perplexing but that's just the way it goes.

If Facebook takes that post down because a libtard got hung by its own throat with its own words, fear not. I have the screen shots and they are here below. The screen shots are up to #17 now with several others from Leila's' Facebook page (that says that she is a new Christian which made her comment about her studying the Scriptures for the past 40 years a lie second to none) and from her private messages because she knew that in the public forum of Facebook, the Lord God was kicking her butt second to none. God gets a little upset when people try to utilize Scripture to support a foolish and impish cad like Obama and calling Obama The Anointed.

No one is called The Anointed but God Himself. Period. End of discussion.

When one utilizes the Word(s) of God to rebuke someone in God's name(s) and they are wrong and in error, what happens to these people? As you will see in message two above, Leila "rebuked me" and said, "get ye behind me Satan" and I was still there and still trying to coax her into reality. But, she saw that I wasn't rebuked so she blocked me. I guess her Scriptures says that's the way to rebuke people that won't listen to Satan, I guess.

I haven't rebuked Leila because there is no reason for it. She is a deceived Christian and needs help and prayer.

Leila says that we are to "pray for our leaders" and that "Obama is The Anointed from God" so any displeasure against Obama is a sin against God". I take exception to that seeing that the Scriptures tells us that we are to pray and support our "leaders" (if we have leaders) when those "leaders" are following God's Laws. I tried to explain this to her that America has no leaders. We have "representatives" that we elect and that We The People are The Leaders of America or, that's the way it was set up.

When we have leaders that are selling God down the river into the quagmire of ignorance and stupidity, how then can we pray for their success? Find that in the Scriptures and I will agree with that. But, you can't find it because it doesn't exist. There is nowhere within the Scriptures where it says that us Christians must play the nice-nice routine with the enemy...ever. The enemy is the enemy and, yes, we can pray that their hearts should change for the better but there are more times, more often than not, that the enemies will be crushed by God Himself.

Isaiah 14:12-21: "How art thou fallen from heaven, O Lucifer, son of the morning! how art thou cut down to the ground, which didst weaken the nations! For thou hast said in thine heart, I will ascend into heaven, I will exalt my throne above the stars of God: I will sit also upon the mount of the congregation, in the sides of the north: I will ascend above the heights of the clouds; I will be like the most High. Yet thou shalt be brought down to hell, to the sides of the pit. They that see thee shall narrowly look upon thee, and consider thee, saying, Is this the man that made the earth to tremble, that did shake kingdoms; That made the world as a wilderness, and destroyed the cities thereof; that opened not the house of his prisoners? All the kings of the nations, even all of them, lie in glory, every one in his own house. But thou art cast out of thy grave like an abominable branch, and as the raiment of those that are slain, thrust through with a sword, that go down to the stones of the pit; as a carcase trodden under feet. Thou shalt not be joined with them in burial, because thou hast destroyed thy land, and slain thy people: the seed of evildoers shall never be renowned. Prepare slaughter for his children for the iniquity of their fathers; that they do not rise, nor possess the land, nor fill the face of the world with cities."

Ezekiel 28:11-19; "Moreover the word of the Lord came unto me, saying, Son of man, take up a lamentation upon the king of Tyrus, and say unto him, Thus saith the Lord God; Thou sealest up the sum, full of wisdom, and perfect in beauty. Thou hast been in Eden the garden of God; every precious stone was thy covering, the sardius, topaz, and the diamond, the beryl, the onyx, and the jasper, the sapphire, the emerald, and the carbuncle, and gold: the workmanship of thy tabrets and of thy pipes was prepared in thee in the day that thou wast created. Thou art the anointed cherub that covereth; and I have set thee so: thou wast upon the holy mountain of God; thou hast walked up and down in the midst of the stones of fire. Thou wast perfect in thy ways from the day that thou wast created, till iniquity was found in thee. By the multitude of thy merchandise they have filled the midst of thee with violence, and thou hast sinned: therefore I will cast thee as profane out of the mountain of God: and I will destroy thee, O covering cherub, from the midst of the stones of fire. Thine heart was lifted up because of thy beauty, thou hast corrupted thy wisdom by reason of thy brightness: I will cast thee to the ground, I will lay thee before kings, that they may behold thee. Thou hast defiled thy sanctuaries by the multitude of thine iniquities, by the iniquity of thy traffick; therefore will I bring forth a fire from the midst of thee, it shall devour thee, and I will bring thee to ashes upon the earth in the sight of all them that behold thee. All they that know thee among the people shall be astonished at thee: thou shalt be a terror, and never shalt thou be any more."

Satan and Hell exist. Heaven and God exist. Anything over and/or above this or under this is barking up the wrong flag pole.

When God has enmity against Satan, how, then, do the people that disgrace God's Words and our Constitution fare within the vision of God seeing that people are lesser beings than one of God's other creations? D they really need to be on the wrong side of God?

Chapter 9 – I Have A Dream[15]

What is the Leftinistra so mired in? Defeat? Hate? Self-loathing? Belief in a rewritten historical account of our nation? Brainwashing?

The Leftinistra hate this country or, they at least hate a form of government built upon a Federal Republic. And, therein, lies a deep-rooted problem. "Liberals" are now "Progressives" and both translate into "socialist" and at worst, "communist" in their pathetic and poisoned rhetoric. Just one example of this can be found at SmolderingMuttBog:

"But here's the deal. Of all the powers in your society, if you live in a democracy, only one is meant to try and help everyone. Only one was set up to do so.

That one is government. By the people, for the people -

those words weren't chosen at random. Government, in the end, is nothing more than a big co-operative."

Obviously, this self-proclaimed "liberal" is so far uneducated as to the make up and framework of this nation and should be disregarded as being an "intellectual" and is to be considered to be a fool's fool. This ignoramus has no earthly clue as to how this nation was constructed and was more than likely taught in the government run re-education camps called Public Schooling and the alleged Higher Learning facilities.

First of all, our Federal Republic was most assuredly not designed to "help everyone". Also, misquoting Lincoln is a sure fire indicator to the level of ignorance and willful bliss of being an idiot. The poor sot omitted "Of The People". Leaving that phrase out is also an indication of the socialist mindset...empty and void of reason, logic and understanding.

The next part is also an indication of the socialist "liberal" stupidity: "Government, in the end, is nothing more than a big co-operative." How sad is that? Pretty sad I am sad to say. If this ignoramus wants to live where the government is a "big co-operative", I suggest the fool pick up stakes and go elsewhere.

However, the key to this pathetic post written by Ian Welsh is this: it thinks we are a "democracy". We are not. The "progressives" would "Rather" we be a democracy but we were founded upon a Federal Republic, plain and simple. In the beginning, the government on the Federal level was not to be Big Brother and to take care of our every need. Quite the contrary.

The Framers were intent on individuality with the State Governments doing the basic "taking care of their citizens". Period. The Framers never intended for the Federal Government to be taking care of all our needs. Period. Perhaps this child should read and study the List of 45? Yes. I do believe the List of 45 is the key to understanding fools like Ian and their pathetic rants of socialist squirrels.

I HAVE A DREAM

I have a Dream. I have a Dream of a Return to The United (still) States of America where True American Patriotism Reigns Supreme. I have a dream where the proponents of the USSA, the United Socialist States of America are defeated and ground into the earth under the boots of True American Patriots. I have a dream where this nation we call America is free of the Anti-Americanists of Code Pink, the Non Answer Coalition, the ACLU and other known socialist and communist groups financing such Marxist, Stalinist, Leninist and Anarchist dogma. I have a dream where the world is free of the Islamic Jihad Menace of which we face is utterly destroyed and the regions they occupy and live are pacified with their blood. I have a dream where Freedom is the New Social Order. I have a dream where the George Soros ilk are trod upon and placed into the Great Abyss of Obscurity in which they belong...for eternity.

I have a dream where the Federal Republic of the United States of America, for which she stands, rules the day and where politicians return to the Delegate Form of Government of which we were founded. I have a dream where the national news agencies actually reports the news without socialist bias and slant...without an agenda, no matter what that agenda may be.

I have a dream where the List of 45 is taught in our schools and in our homes and most importantly, within the Local, State and Federal Governments to remind them of what almost transpired in this country as we slept. The list was presented to Congress in 196[3] and how soon have we forgotten the threats from within.

I have a dream that the Silent Majority will turn off their televisions and get involved in the future of their nation before all is lost. I have a dream where True American Patriots rise up and say, "I am mad as hell and I'm not going to take this anymore!" I have a dream where the American Microwave Mentality is no more. I have dream where the average American Memory Span and Attention Span is longer than a week...perhaps even develop an ability and a desire for long-term memory and attention spans. Is this asking for too much? Perhaps but a man can dream.

Won't you join me?

Further reading:
Democracy v Federal Republic...Which Are We?

Sounds catchy, doesn't it? Martin Luther King, Jr (a Republican by the way) who was supported by Republicans (and Democrats fought him by the way), stood and gave the famous speech that is known as I Have A Dream. Obama used that anniversary of the famous MLK speech delivery to reveal to the world what kind of a fraud he truly is, complete with Greek Temple Styrofoam pillars. He announced his dream of bringing back slavery because the Democrat Party has a deep resentment of the collapse of legalized slavery. The Democrat Party has a long and infamous history of racism, slavery, bigotry, sexism and many other heinous "isms".

The Democrats fought the Civil Rights Movement. The Democrats created the KKK. The Democrats fought the end of slavery in the 1800s. The Democrats thrive on keeping racism and all the other ugly "isms" alive and well to feed on the down-trodden and keep them dependent of the government dole-outs of meager subsistence and subservience. It is a matter of public record. Ask Senator Byrd. He knows full well, him being a former Grand Kleagle and all.

However, my dream is much deeper than Martin Luther King Jr's dream was in my opinion. I am not taking away from his dream at all because it was a noble dream and a heartfelt dream and a matter-of-fact dream which had to come about for this nation's survival and reputation. Unfortunately, the Leftinistra in our land that dwell amongst us all stole his dream, made it their own and raped it. I laugh in scornful disdain every time I hear a member of the Leftinistra use his name in vain to further their political agendas of oppression, fear and hate.

On Sunday, April 27, 2008 at 4:35PM, I published an article under this same title, I Have A Dream. It was met with the usual fanfare of derision and scorn from the anti-Americanists we now recognize as the Leftinistra, the armies of the socialist liberals in this nation. Some call them AINOs...Americans In Name Only.

If you so desire, feel free to click on the article I wrote over a year ago. If you read it, you will find that something strange is happening in America. Americans are awakening from their slumber - a self-induced trance evidently coming from their willful suspensions of their disbelief of what has taken place in this nation under their very noses. I read it again this evening and early morning hours amazed at the uncanny predictions. I was going to repost that article here but it would merely detract from this article...my New Dream. I don't know if it truly is a dream per se. It could very well be a wishful thought. At any rate, as I witnessed what transpired in Iran over the weekend and after witnessing the total absence of reason of the responses given by Biden and two days later Obama, I recalled this dream that I have discussed many times in private conversations and in conversations on the Blog Talk Radio circuits.

I was going to put the dream to paper and publish it when I received an email message from Pat Dollard with a link to a story from Iran: "Iran's Day Of Destiny: A Million Brave Iranians Defy Death And Bring Shame To Cowardly Anti-Obama Americans". The title alone speaks volumes. The time for talk is done. The time for negotiating with the enemies amongst us has past us by. It is in fact time for action. Hopefully, that action will be peaceful...it will be from our side of the fence but most assuredly, it won't be peaceful from the Leftinistra. The public record of that is plainly and painfully obvious.

Nearly ONE MILLION proud Iranians stood up and were counted. The Second Iranian Revolution just might come to pass. Then again, it might not. However, they arose to the occasion and spoke out against the tyrannical dictators that are soon to plunge their Nation into war with other Nations or war within its own borders. Is that our destiny? If we do not stop the Marxist political coup in this nation, the answer will be in fact a woeful HELL YES!

Comment:

"Just remember Us Shameful Cowardly Anti-Obama Americans, still have our guns and ammunition. Our Forefathers, knew a time will come; that time has not arrived Yet."

So, without further ado...

I Have A Dream

I have a vision, a dream, perhaps a portent...not exactly sure what to call it. However, just imagine people showing up in DC or State and local capitals, no flags, no colorful banners, no signs, "normal" attire, no chanting, no loud horns, no sirens, no cat calls...nothing but silence.

Standing silently, shoulder to shoulder with our backs to the Halls of Congress as we surround them with our numbers. Standing silently, shoulder to shoulder with our backs to the now renamed Marxist House as we surround them with our numbers. Standing silently, no idle chit-chat...no chatter at all. Just standing there surrounding the buildings...our backs to them all.

The same can be done across this Nation's State government hide outs of the criminals that defy the United States Constitution and all that we were founded upon - freedom, liberty, life and free choice to be the individuals we are and live our lives within the confines of constitutionally derived Law and Order and not some declared and contrived emergency as our history reveals time and time again as shredding our very existence.

When asked questions, we do not answer - no eye contact, staring out beyond whomever stands before us and piercing through them as if they did not exist.

Standing in silence, ne'er a whisper, rain, shine, sleet, snow, hurricane, tornado.

Standing in silence for an hour or so, thirty minutes, ten - whatever we can bear - and then simply walking away, vanishing into the city.

And then returning to repeat the process at unpredictable times and intervals.

These are not scheduled "rallies" so no permits will be needed.

Spontaneous, silent defiance.

Genesis 37:5; "And Joseph dreamed a dream, and he told it his brethren: and they hated him yet the more."

Jeremiah 23:28; "The prophet that hath a dream, let him tell a dream; and he that hath my word, let him speak my word faithfully. What is the chaff to the wheat? saith the LORD."

Joel 2:28; "And it shall come to pass afterward, that I will pour out my spirit upon all flesh; and your sons and your daughters shall prophesy, your old men shall dream dreams, your young men shall see visions:"

Acts 2:17; "And it shall come to pass in the last days, saith God, I will pour out of my Spirit upon all flesh: and your sons and your daughters shall prophesy, and your young men shall see visions, and your old men shall dream dreams:"

Yes, I have dreams and, yes, we are in the End Times.

Chapter 10 – Democracy vs A Republic[16,17,18]

The below entries are from 8 entries at my web site, *The Snooper Report,* and I have contained those posts to three here in this book.

Democracy...What Is It?

Thursday, March 01, 2007 4:47 AM

This is my take...I am just an old warrior, a grunt.

Feel free to correct me and/or leave comments...I am all ears...

What is democracy? What is Liberty? We hear all kinds of

references to both these days, don't we? The terms get thrown away and I fear that the majority of Americans haven't a clue, really, what either term means. We won't even get into the terms Federal Republic or Democratic Republic and related terminology. According to the Webster's Ninth New Collegiate Dictionary, democracy has been given the defined as "government by the people; especially: rule of the majority", among a few others. What does majority rule mean and why is that an important aspect of democracy? Is majority rule relevant? If so then why? According to the same dictionary previously mentioned, majority rule has been given the definition as, "a political principle providing that a majority usually constituted by 50% plus one of an organized group will have the power to make decisions binding upon the whole." Wow; such a gaggle of words. We can gather from the definitions of Democracy and Majority Rule that the principles derived from them pertain to a tool whereby decisions can be made and applied or enforced.

With that in mind, is Democracy a good thing or a bad thing? Consider this; you like strawberry milkshakes but the majority has voted and taken the decision as to whether you should like strawberry milkshakes under consideration. The majority votes that it will be vanilla milkshakes and the strawberry milkshakes will no longer be available. The same process can be applied to every aspect of your life. Is this good or is it bad? For you, the strawberry milkshake drinker, it is bad. You are in the minority so you lose that particular choice. The decision process has been removed from you. For the majority, there is no more issue. Vanilla milkshakes it is. That "sounds" a little like tyranny, doesn't it? Does this mean that Democracy is a form of tyranny?

Yes, it is. However, this form of tyranny is an elected type of tyranny. What then, is tyranny? It is back to the dictionary for a definition, "oppressive power exerted by government." Really? We just had an election and the majority voted for vanilla milkshakes. The majority rules in a Democratic society so why is this considered to be tyrannical? This issue isn't as simple as some would lead us to believe.

The Father of our Constitution, James Madison had this to say about a pure Democracy, "there is nothing to check the inducement to sacrifice the weaker party or the obnoxious individual." So, then, we may gather that a Democracy, in its purest form can lead to tyranny. So, is Democracy good then? Ask John Adams. He had this gem to express, "Remember, democracy never lasts long. It soon wastes, exhausts and murders itself. There was never a democracy yet that did not commit suicide."

Other wise men have made observations about democracy and several have compared democracy to a republic and have determined that the differences between the two are similar to the differences between chaos and order. Isn't that a wondrous commentary to ponder? People of the world and world leaders prattle on about Democracy and all they want is tyranny, chaos and order? This can sound rather contradictory can it not? Why would other peoples want this?

You see, our Founding Fathers were really smart men. They had lived through various forms of government and watched many come and go. They knew the pitfalls and the snares and the traps. Unfortunately, our modern leaders have lost their way.

Our Founding Fathers had every intention on protecting the people of the new Nation of America. They did not want a tyrannical form of government. They did not want a king. They did not want a dictator. They intended to create a republican form of government. We will need to define this form of government so, it is back to the dictionary, "a government in which supreme power resides in a body of citizens entitled to vote and is exercised by elected officers and representatives responsible to them and governing according to law." This is a far cry from Democracy is it not?

Personally, I don't know why our politicians in this country as well as others make a big deal over Democracy. It is certainly superior to Socialism or Communism but we will discuss those issues another day. Would it not be better to spread our Founding Fathers' dream and experiment? Yes it would. However, we would have to return to it in order to proclaim it and spread the good news around.

That brings us to Liberty. What is Liberty? It is the "freedom to do as one pleases (anarchy) and quality or state of being free and free from arbitrary or despotic control." Our form of government as envisioned by our Founding Fathers was a Federal Republic, ruling over the "various states" and ensuring continuity and protection from foreign and domestic enemies.

It was a combination of Democracy, Tyranny, Republican, Anarchy and Liberty. Combine them all into one form and you achieve a Federal Republic where the PEOPLE govern and the politicians carry out the demands of the PEOPLE, not the other way around. The people are free to CHANGE the government at will. (Remember that.) Combining these five elements and deriving law and order, a healthy society will emerge.

Today, in America, the politicians have become the

governing body and "We The People" are their serfs. We have become a form of government our Founding Fathers feared the most. The people are no longer the ruling body.

Democracy...What Is It Addendum

Tuesday, March 06, 2007 12:55 AM

This writing is an adjunct to a post I made which can be found in the featured post section under "Democracy...What Is It".

I have read on the blogs at Townhall and elsewhere, where several terminologies are either being exaggerated, abused and/or misrepresented.

I have been hearing we are a "Democratic Republic". I have been hearing that we are a "Democracy". I have been hearing that we are a "Republic". It all started when an author posted the "Atheist Democracy" article. That was a good article, btw.

However, my article "Democracy...What Is It" was more or less a recap of 200+ years of history of this nation. It is a shortened version of the book I am writing and hopefully, one day, in my lifetime, I will finish the bloody thing.

With that being said, I will post here a tid-bit of data that will explain in not so much boring detail, the gist of what a Federal Republic is, in laymen's terms.

The United States was founded as a Federal Republic. This means that is was to be a representative form of government. Many people do not know what this entails.

There are three forms of "representation".

First, there is the Trustee form. This is where the elected official, theoretically, listens to the constituents and is trusted to use their best judgments to make decisions. (not a good plan)

Second, there is the Delegate representative who votes the way their constituents would want them to vote, whether or not the representative agrees with the majority of the constituents. (majority rule)

Third, there is the Politico representative which, flip-flops between the Delegate and Trustee forms of representation, depending on the issue(s). (not a good plan)

It is the Delegate form that is what the Framers had intended and it worked that way up until FDR. From FDR and on, our representation went to hell and hasn't recovered yet. This form is what creates accountability in politics and we have not had much of that in decades, have we? Are we currently being represented by Delegates? In my estimation, most certainly not.

The Trustee form is what lazy and uninterested Sheeple choose to live under and their "rights" can be stripped away because the Elected One "hears" them but tends to "ignore" them. Tyranny is the result.

The Politico form is a mish-mash form of socialized "keep-them-in-the-dark and feed them fish eyes" representation. There is ZERO accountability.

The Federal Republic was making a come-back during the Reagan and Bush years but was reverted back to the socialistic ways of FDR when Clinton gained control of the American Helm.

This must be reversed before it is too late. Should a Leftinistra gain the Throne of American politics, we will be very close to another American Civil War. Our country has not been this split since 1861. I make this statement because our country has not been this split since 1861. And, look what that bred.

Our Founding Fathers and others speak out

Democracy: a government of the masses. Authority derived thru mass meeting or any other form of direct expression. Results in Mobacracy. Attitude toward property is communist - negating property rights. Attitude toward law is that the will of the majority shall regulate, whether it be based upon deliberation or governed by passion. prejudice and impulse without restraint or regard to consequences. Results in demagoguism, license, agitation, discontent, anarchy.

Republic: Authority is derived thru the election by the people of public officials best fitted to represent them. Attitude toward law is the administration of justice in accord with fixed principles and established evidence, with a strict regard to consequences. A greater number of citizens and extent of territory may be brought within its compass. Avoids the dangerous extreme of either tyranny or mobacracy. Results in statesmanship, liberty, reason, justice, contentment and progress. Is the standard form of government throughout the world.

Benjamin Franklin: When the people find that they can vote themselves money that will herald the end of the republic.

Alexander Hamilton, Federalist Papers: We are a Republican Government, Real liberty is never found in despotism or in the extremes of democracy...it has been observed that a pure democracy if it were practicable would be the most perfect government. Experience has proved that no position is more false than this. The ancient democracies in which the people themselves deliberated never possessed one good feature of government. Their very character was tyranny; their figure deformity.

John Adams: Democracy never lasts long. It soon wastes, exhausts, and murders itself. There never was a democracy yet that did not commit suicide.

Thomas Jefferson: A democracy is nothing more than mob rule, where 51% of the people may take away the rights of the other 49%.

James Madison: Democracies have ever been spectacles of turbulence and contention; have ever been found incompatible with personal security or the rights of property; and have in general been as short in their lives as they have been violent in their death.

John Quincy Adams: The experience of all former ages had shown that of all human governments, democracy was the most unstable, fluctuating and short-lived.

Thomas Jefferson: The democracy will cease to exist when you take away from those who are willing to work and give to those who would not.

Benjamin Franklin (maybe): Democracy is two wolves and a lamb voting on what to have for lunch. Liberty is a well-armed lamb contesting the vote.

James Madison: Democracy was the right of the people to choose their own tyrant.

John Adams: That the desires of the majority of the people are often for injustice and inhumanity against the minority, is demonstrated by every page of the history of the world.

Thomas Jefferson: All, too, will bear in mind this sacred principle, that through the will of the majority is in all cases to prevail, that will, to be rightful, must be reasonable; that the minority possess their equal rights, which equal laws must protect, and to violate would be oppression.

John Witherspoon: Pure democracy cannot subsist long nor be carried far into the departments of state - it is very subject to caprice and the madness of popular rage.

James Madison: We may define a republic to be - a government which derives all its powers directly or indirectly from the great body of the people, and is administered by persons holding their offices during pleasure for a limited period, or during good behavior. It is essential to such a government that it be derived from the great body of the society, not from an inconsiderable proportion or a favored class of it: otherwise a handful of tyrannical nobles, exercising their oppressions by a delegation of their powers, might aspire to the rank of republicans and claim for their government the honorable title of republic.

John Marshall: Between a balanced republic and a democracy, the difference is like that between order and chaos.

Oscar Wilde: Democracy means simply the bludgeoning of the people by the people for the people.

Winston Churchill: The best argument against democracy is a five minute conversation with the average voter.

Sydney J Harris: Democracy is the only system that persists in asking the powers that be whether they are the powers that ought to be.

G. K., Chesterton: Democracy means government by the uneducated, while aristocracy means government by the badly educated.

George Bernard Shaw: Democracy substitutes election by the incompetent many for appointment by the corrupt few.

Dr Laurence J Peter: Democracy is a process by which the people are free to choose the man who will get the blame.

Alan Coren: Democracy consists of choosing your dictators after they've told you what you think it is you want to hear.

Karl Marx: Democracy is the road to socialism.

And there you have it. I have nearly 500 quotes from our Founding Fathers to clearly debunk the retarded liberals that say we are a Democracy.

So, there you have it. This nation, no matter which liberal in the DNC and the GOP says, is a Republic and not a pathetic democracy. A democracy cannot adhere to a Judeo-Christian ethic which is why this nation is in the peril of which it is in which is why I wrote the book *The Biblical Basis of the American Federal Constitution*[19], now in its second edition. If this nation, under the current aspects of the politicians, will not follow Christ, they are in fact following Satan and moors the pity.

Isaiah 9:6; "For unto us a child is born, unto us a son is given: and the government shall be upon his shoulder: and his name shall be called Wonderful, Counsellor, The mighty God, The everlasting Father, The Prince of Peace."

Isaiah 9:7; "Of the increase of his government and peace there shall be no end, upon the throne of David, and upon his kingdom, to order it, and to establish it with judgment and with justice from henceforth even for ever. The zeal of the LORD of hosts will perform this."

Isaiah 22:21; "And I will clothe him with thy robe, and strengthen him with thy girdle, and I will commit thy government into his hand: and he shall be a father to the inhabitants of Jerusalem, and to the house of Judah."

2 Peter 2:10; "But chiefly them that walk after the flesh in the lust of uncleanness, and despise government. Presumptuous are they, selfwilled, they are not afraid to speak evil of dignities."

Our "old" government was conceived in Christ and our "new" government is conceived in Satan. Pity.

FOOTNOTES

1: http://www.snooperreport.com/snooper-report/2009/2/5/live-free-or-die.html

2: http://www.snooperreport.com/snooper-report/2009/2/17/live-free-or-die-trying.html

3: http://www.snooperreport.com/snooper-report/2009/2/20/states-sovereignty-or-live-free-or-die.html

4: http://snooperreport.com/snooper-report/2010/5/26/titles-of-nobility-and-honor-the-missing-13th-amendment.html

5: http://snooperreport.com/snooper-report/2010/6/4/our-founding-document-wasnt-set-in-stone-for-a-reason.html

6: Good audio segment, http://snooperreport.com/snooper-report/2009/7/4/be-it-known-attention-unconstitutional-congress.html

7: http://snooperreport.com/snooper-report/2010/2/9/do-birthers-rock-and-roll-or-stop-and-drool.html

8: http://www.snooperreport.com/snooper-report/2009/11/24/we-didnt-start-this-goddamn-war.html

9: Madison's notes, http://snooperreport.com/storage/constitution/madisons-notes/intro%20to%20madison%27s%20notes.jpg

10: Madison's notes, http://snooperreport.com/storage/constitution/madisons-notes/james%20madison%20flag%20capital.jpg

11: Barbary Coast War, http://memory.loc.gov/ammem/collections/jefferson_papers/mtjprece.html

12: http://snooperreport.com/snooper-report/2009/4/30/democrats-and-terrorists-whats-the-difference.html

13: http://snooperreport.com/snooper-report/2009/11/27/the-american-liberal-marxist-sociopath-and-the-terrorists-is.html

14: http://snooperreport.com/snooper-report/2013/8/3/when-satan-has-beguiled-the-ignorant-or-when-liberal-christi.html

15: http://snooperreport.com/snooper-report/2009/6/16/i-have-a-dream.html

16: http://snooperreport.com/say-no-to-jihad/2007/5/28/democracywhat-is-it.html

17: http://snooperreport.com/say-no-to-jihad/2007/5/28/democracywhat-is-it-adendum.html

18: http://snooperreport.com/snooper-report/2007/7/1/democracy.html

19: The Biblical Basis for the American Federal Constitution, http://www.lulu.com/shop/publius-marcus/the-biblical-basis-of-the-american-federal-constitution/paperback/product-21563788.html

20: http://snooperreport.com/snooper-report/2009/11/22/good-vs-evilit-is-your-choice.html

www.ingramcontent.com/pod-product-compliance
Lightning Source LLC
Chambersburg PA
CBHW020337290526
45785CB00005B/2067